ONE LESS RIVER

One Less River

by Terry Blackhawk

Mayapple Press 2019

Published by   Mayapple Press
                  362 Chestnut Hill Road
                  Woodstock, NY 12498
                  mayapplepress.com

ISBN 978-1-936419-89-0
Library of Congress Control Number 2019903811

For Peter Markus

Farsi translations by Soodabeh Saeidnia.

Cover design by Judith Kerman; cover art by Neil Frankenhauser. Cover photo of author by Kennen White; bio photo of author by Desiree Cooper. Book designed and typeset by Judith Kerman with titles in Lithos Pro and text in Californian FB.

CONTENTS

Greet yourself
In your thousand other forms
As you mount the hidden tide and travel
Home.

—*Hafiz*

I.

THE DOOR

Why is it lately closed to me?
I will not complain. These grasses share the light.
They bend and catch the wind gracefully.

The dance I missed, too shy, the other night—
I wish I'd gone to the perfumery.
A sauna's slats, so fragrant, wrap me now.
I've crawled into a barrel on the hill.

NAUSET

She walked toward the dunes, toward a house that she thought was in the dunes, but it had been gone years before she got to where it once had been. She had read about it, envying the naturalist his small light-filled room with sixteen windows in all directions and the weathered planks up on stilts over the dune, and she had imagined the wind rattling against the wooden shutters and thought about how it would be to run her hands across such shutters. She imagined they would be silky to the touch, smoothed for so many years by salt and spray and wind, and the many panes of the sixteen windows would be transparent to the world, giving views onto the tops of dunes where warblers dipped and surfaced from inside the vegetation, the beach roses and heather and other low-growing bushes that clung there. Below, there would be clumps of dune grass sweeping and making circles in the sand around them, and hermit crabs and other creatures without backbones inhabiting the burrows they excavated. The beach had stretched for miles and she had covered many of them, walking determinedly over the hard sand that had blown smooth but was still damp from the receding tide. Terns and sandpipers had flown up at her approach, standing at water's edge and facing out to sea single file and unmoving until she neared them and they flew up to settle again in the same formation a little ways down the shore,

reminding her of how once, on another beach, years before, a nesting mother tern had hovered over her head and dived toward her hat, the floppy green felt hat, which she wore all the time then and that she waved the bird off with since she had not seen its eggs in the sand at her feet. On that long ago dune, she had built herself a dwelling, with washed up planks and driftwood for walls and a tarp that she had carried in her backpack as a roof over her head and a sleeping bag on the ground. She had some hard bread and dried fruit for sustenance and enough water if she were careful with it, and her little dwelling nestled snugly down into the dune so that only the top of it caught the breezes. She could turn over in her sleeping bag and see the sun rising red over the water and swim naked later in the day in the waves and walk along the beach and make things for herself, weaving a shade for the western side of her dwelling out of grasses and fronds she collected in the scrub woods and bushes farther in from the shore. She read some poems and wrote and drew in her daybook by day and built a small fire at night, and time, except for a small plane that one day buzzed quite low, was unbroken and calm. After several days of this, the wind and the grass and the waves began to sing to her so she waited for the next sunrise and then packed her backpack and dismantled the driftwood structure and took down the mat of woven grasses and headed off on the long walk down the island toward the outermost station where she could find a train that would take her back into the city.

Overheard Among the Arthropods

And I said to myself: dwell in your shell.
—Moondog

i. Hermit crabs

Occasionally it is amusing
one of us announces   antennae
clicking   claws
barely touching the sand
to recognize ourselves without
these shells

and think of the pulpy
creatures who used to live
inside

ii. Jellyfish

No shell necessary
when one is gelatinous
      carried by
and through   currents   *così così*
barely visible
in the diffuse light

Beached now my shifting
shape recalls
bubbles blown through
mucilage squeezed
from a tube

strings sticky and shiny
as these tentacles
now dissolving
into sand

iii. Driftwood

One is attractive
enough in
       retrospect

Even washed up on shore
genes determine the degree
       of polish

Take these whorls   whirls
some resultant mix
of experience and inclination

shadow and sheen

iv. Scarab

Would you like to come
scrawl
with me   we
could be artists whose
signatures   get   left behind

Desire takes such droll
design   think of antennae
as bits of wing

v. Submersibles

We bury ourselves
above the line of the tide

feel the sole of your
boot press   back from
our   roof   a quick
water-logged   medium

              this

tensile   suspension
between one ground
and another

vi. Hermits, ii

Disjointed   angular   we
                              inhabit
the shells of others
although some unity inheres
our curved moves   our arcs
of yearning

Your amusement confirms us
even if you ignore the shyness
even if what emerges
                              is a claw

THE EXTINCT FRESH WATER MUSSELS OF THE DETROIT RIVER

for Kathryne Lindberg (1951-2010)

These are gone: *the deer-toe maple leaf, the fat*
mucket, the snuffbox, the rainbow shell. Here, still,

the rusted manhole cover and the chipping paint,
the lights and arches of the elegant bridge,

all coated no doubt then in ice. Here the breeze,
here the freighters but not the car. Quiet as it's kept,

it's no secret the keys were left in the ignition.

Absence makes the fond heart wander, the mind
meander, the river to swallow its flow—

the self-same river, the self-same self, even the one
that knew better, the self that knew better

than to pick up a phony ten-dollar bill folded
to disguise some evangelical come-hither.

Come hither, said the bridge.

Little earwig mussel, pimpleback, northern riffle shell,
something lacy yet along the rim.

In the print gallery a dry-point fox in outline
("Running Fox," R. Sintemi, Germany, 1944) floats
as if on the surface of a river, water swelling upward
on the verge of breaking up its lines—

Did you float, dear bat-out-of-hell, dear gnashing teeth—
the pointed ears, the flowing tail outlined on water not water,

on paper not paper, on the not-water before there only was
water, where we are floating now, as over a great uncertainty,
a mirroring surface that hides as much as it reveals.

No more *rayed bean, purple warty back. O fragile paper shell*—
Where was the artist in 1944? What did he do in 1939?

You would have wanted to know.

DOWN IN DETROIT

Help me! I live in Detroit.
Sign taped to a tip cup on the popcorn counter,
Maple Art Theater, Bloomfield Hills, MI—2003

Remember when the flight attendant had us prepare
for landing in "Honolu...oops, Detroit"
and the whole plane laughed?
And did I tell you the one about the ex-
Michigander who turned her back on me
& pointedly bestowed her life story (Border Collies
and Harry Potter included) on another woman
waiting for the Napa Shuttle after I winced
& replied yes, yes, **in** Detroit, I live
IN Detroit. Or the librarian from Rochester Hills:
his "You live down in Detroit?" still echoes
down, down, down.
                        Tough enough to love
this town without the shocked looks, dropped
jaws of fellow citizens who assume whiteness
unites as they eye you, reassessing instantly. Still,
"The D"—dear "D"—must have some magic in it.
How else explain the doubled take, the suddenly shed
disguise? In less than an eye-blink, I've had men
switch from flirt to default mode, their mental
U-turns screeching with chagrin. Such power
in a word: to make a person give himself away.
Dee-troit, *day–twah,* **strait in French, place where waters**
move swiftly.

CITIZEN POET

And so are some souls like stars.
—Johnny Cash

And so here we stand, one foot in your *Bodega Republic*,
The other reaching for Alpha Centauri or wherever it is
You've migrated to, crossing some cosmic Mason-Dixon line
Between the blues and eternity, submerged now into waves of light
Like the Atlantic you loved, the amber waves of grain you refused
To revere. Street corner poet, denizen of grandeur
And elevators, bebop, jazz, addiction, and diggerido,
Haunted by hanging trees and the last outposts,
Now that you are in the shooting stars, may we never forget
The first beats you gave us: *the music that comes*
From the steady racket of the wheels
Tracking over the rails. Today, I learned how gray
Becomes the blues: you overlay the paint. Each alphabet is a sign,
A destination. Each word, an encaustic target. You overlay the paint.
You apply the heat. It's not only artists do this, Space
Man. Which, of course, you knew. The principle of collection
Is to accept, accept: the doo-wop, the hip hop, the both/and, thumb-
Popping tabla-tapping rhyme-junkie, alliterating your traumas,
Adding those extra syllables just for the joy of the count, turning
Towering terror into questions and light, and yes, call it—magic:
Some kind of conjure to help us to overcome, lift up and to hold.
Through the sonic screen and the oversized close-ups,
What you channeled channels still, to us here, where here and there,
Possible and impossible, merge as one. Oh wild and wiley—
Your reverberations from Space beam on,
Widening the orbit of you, dearest mindful one, beloved wall-
Mender, molasses voice, kindest heart, Oh ju-ju man, our Lazarus—

Our peace.

For Sekou Sundiata (1948-2007)

THE WOODCOCK

Weary of the daily terror I turn
to the mystic body of the bird. A woodcock
I found *crackling the twigs* and ivy,
barely escaped from a cat's clumsy claws.
I feared for the odd angle of its wing,
the surprised flopping it made there,
but I did not fear the extreme length
of its beak or the eyes popping diametrically
on either side of its head. I loved the feathers'
deckled edges and the light weight it made
as I scooped it up and put it, *limpsy and weak*,
into an old canvas book bag, and when I
released it from that soft *safe space*
some time later, out on Belle Isle, I missed it
at once, as one would miss a friend.
It whirred straight up, explosively,
toward freedom on the other side of the river,
its pulse now gone from my hands.

ابیا*

تری بلک هاوک

خسته از وحشت روزانه

من به جسم عارفانه یک پرنده بر می گردم بنام "ابیا"

شاخه ها و پیچک ها را شکننده یافتم

و به سختی از چنگال دست و پا چلفتی یک گربه گریختم

از زاویه عجیب بال آن پرنده ترسیدم

که با صدای شگفت انگیزی فرو می افتاد

اما از منقار بسیار بلندش هراسی نداشتم

و یا از چشمانش که جداگانه در هر طرف سرش می چرخید

من عاشق لبه های برش خورده پرهای سبک او شدم

وقتی که او را – در حالیکه سست و ضعیف بود – بر داشتم

و در کوله پشتی پارچه ای قدیمی ام گذاشتم

و سپس او را از آن فضای امن و نرم رها کردم

خارج از این جزیره، وبه یکباره برایش دلتنگ شدم

درست همانطور که برای یک دوست دلتنگ می شوی

اوچون تیری رها شده، مستقیما بسوی آزادی پرواز کرد

به سوی آزادی در سمت دیگر رودخانه

دستانم از ضربانش خالی شده

نُت متن حم: وودکاک، خروس جنگلی یا اینا نام پرنده ای که حک است که در جنگلهای اروپا و

21

ONE LESS RIVER

for Blair (1967-2011)

Okay, so you'd try anything, and you were
always ready to go—to South Africa, Siberia,
New York—barely two cents in your pocket, a guitar for the subway,
a laugh to get you through the night.

And you'd ride anything. You disdained
cowboys, but when the cowboy says how he can't resist
                "...that unexplainable feeling
that makes me go get on bulls. It's like everything just stops...
the world has stopped spinning...at that point in time"
                    —it's you I hear: dancing, riding the line.

Eternal stoppage. Perpetual spin.

Last night the moon was a coin, a relief
of wings, a scarab
beaten gold, 'rounded' or rendered,
to place on your eyelids, forever now.

Today a darker fuzz belies the sun.
How dreary myth becomes.
Forget this channel of regret, gospel coinage,
tedious juke joints, tankers heading south.

Dear ventriloquist: don't move your lips.
Listen to the hermits—
antennae clicking   claws   barely touching   the sand

Perpetual stoppage.   Eternal spin.
Put those shells in your pocket.
Make it one less river to cross, a second time.

THE IVORY GULL UNDER THE BRIDGE OVER THE FLINT RIVER

The insignificant is as big to me as any.
—*Walt Whitman*

"Near threatened"—"accidental"—the gull
winged, meandered its ivory way
thousands of miles from the Arctic here
to Flint, Michigan, where it sat on
the dam's spillway, *insignificant*
yet *as big* to us as an omen.
Hundreds flocked to photograph, pluck its
glimmering name from the slimy dark
concrete where the poisoned water flows.

No less than the journey-work of stars,
bright migrant I'm still yearning to see—
or one like it: a Razor-billed Auk
or Snowy Owl, the pristine ice fields
they hail from receding now while all
the bird-whiles I've savored shimmer in
memory and grief against this bleak
industrial stage my friend captured
on film, the bird later found dead there.

Sibley: "the one pure white gull, plumage
dazzlingly white, often very tame.
Voice, a mewing, high whistle strongly
descending." Am I wrong to think of
Eurydice at Hades's throne, bird
as halcyon respite? *Great monsters
are lying low. In vain the buzzard
houses herself with the sky.* Never mind
the sickened children of the town.

TALLAHATCHIE

Peonies petal-shake in heavy
Rain propped up by their companion-
Able fence. Does structure help to
Hold the deluge back? Let no scythe hack
A single sweet head down
Nor wind a wire nor leave Chicago child unhorsed.
His memory is a river that
Spreads mist still. Distant whistler, little
Fall of bloom, droplets, eyes that saw no foe.

R.I.P. Emmett Till

STILLNESS IN THE AIR—BETWEEN

What fresh dangers tap against the black window?
—Desiree Cooper

You learn a certain wariness.   You learn
your late night descent   to the chair in its circle
            of lamplight   may be your only move
given the hour   the heavy weather
your clammy skin—   and you find yourself
wishing for an opposite (but still parallel)   other
set of stairs   than the one   you just padded down
                so carefully in your bare feet.
                You turn and turn
the radio dial   but there is some
        atmospheric disturbance   and the small green light
hits no fixed station   misses   a ninth inning
or an eleventh   cannot find   Mahler's Third
or the preacher   whooping   saving souls
                    somewhere down in Alabama.

All you hear   is the crackling background
        whatever it may be—   the edge of the expanding universe
the sound   of your mind meeting itself   a static
        film   bees   working over a meadow.
Curtains move   and you sigh the way a room sighs as a door
                    opens   and   adjusts
the pressure—   Wind forces the windows.   The harmonics
of the house hit   the exact pitch of an empty
crayon box you'd hold in your mouth   and blow into just to hear it
        squeal   to feel the vibration   against your lips
as a slight cellular itch—
                    Then the lightning—   before
the storm heaves in upon you—   leaves you   quivering/searching
for an opening to duck into   a burrow
        you've abandoned—   somewhere
                            to begin
as difficult—

II.

She Awakens in a Town by the Sea

The street, milling all night. Old lace—
faces peeking out into drifts of blossoms,

drifts of bloom. Tell me about yourself, Sweetie.
Everything you say may be held against you.

Drifts of blossoms, studies of bloom.
Or boas. Boas and other entanglements.

The auditions go on regardless.
Mammatus, *Mami Wata*—clouds

begin to break. When she steps outside,
a soprano's song saturates the air.

Shards of shells on the walk beneath her
feet. Gardens tuning up in a minor

key. Before their petals fall away, she will lift
a shattered glass.

A gull coasts over the jetty. Drifts
of blossoms, curtains of bloom.

PROVINCETOWN, AUGUST

She listened seven ways at once, walked to the end
of Pier Two, then back again along Pier One.

Humming, this Protea, dallying. Stuffin' gone
outta her then, innit, doll? Now she picks up her favorite

pen and puts it to the paper she likes best. Jetsam
bobbing there along the shore. No caterwauling

creature hubbubbin' about the wharf no more; a bit
o'sea cucumber wrack but a sheen to 'er, all the same.

Once, a broken sandal, the dusty road past
a thick-walled church and when you opened a door...

All her life she's lived *frugally, on surprise.*
She loved the click of tiles across

a game board, chances smooth in her hand.
Her arm listed

slightly to the left, and delicate, like the cat
balanced on pilings outside Harpooners'

last night, or the distant music of tiny spoons
on porcelain cups stirring tea.

Even so, she'll give it one more mumbledy-peg.
Before whales begin to feed, they cast bubble nets

through the water, spreading haloes upward in luminous
turquoise rings.

CONTEMPLATING THE WAFER

She is so immersed as to be almost
                    dissolvable   soluble
a hostess of dissolution
Think of her as a wafer, semi-
permeable the way
her arms move through the ambiguous
light   there are a few waves from the nearby lane
and she likes her body like this
tight as a corkscrew plowing through
this element counting back and forth the laps mount into time
passing the passerines come to roost and procreate migrate
                    and return
the globe is marked by their landings and wanderings
an entire host melts within her she is the taste the sacrifice
sacred on the tongue.

GRIEF, IN VENICE

reveals itself, in stages,
illumining your lack
of balance, your disjointed
hands. Steadfast, it dissolves
at your approach, gives you
stones to trip over, over
and over, pins you anew on
the precipice of childhood
with a *carnevale* mask
fixed to your face. Listen for it
in the gulls' catlike cries,
the convent bells—their grating
sounds—or water taxis, market crowds.
You will find it *dappertutto*
in ripples of light
off the canals or that bird
you can finally see, near a geranium-filled
window box, singing from its cage.

اندوه، در ونیز

تری بلک هاوک

خود را طی مراحلی نشان می دهد

عدم تعادلت را آشکار می کند

دستهایت که بی مفصل است

استوار که باشی، این مشکل با رویکرد تو حل می شود

سنگهایی را به تو می دهد

که سفر کنی دوباره، دوباره و دوباره

تو را به شیوه ای جدید

در پرتگاه کودکیت میخکوب می کند

با صورتکی از یک کارناوال

که بر صورتت نهاده

به صدای گریه مرغان دریایی گوش بسپار

که چون نالیدن گربه است

زنگهای صومعه ـ صداهای گوشخراش-

و تاکسی های آبی، شلوغی بازار

می توانی این را در همه جا بیابی

در امواج نور

در کانال ها و یا در آن پرنده

که در نهایت می توانی ببینی، در نزدیکی پنجره ای

که با گل های شمعدانی پوشیده شده، در قفسش آواز می خواند

ICE MUSIC

ice melt ice lace ice
breaking up upstream
coming down from up
north in variegated
quilts of floes
no *instant's act* this
crumbling   an entire
season sends broken
continents our way
once-miles-wide chunks break
and bob or push up
against the shore
in spun sugar turrets
they rise fall glistening
dissolving   ice lace
ice music   I seem
to hear a tremolo
in the trees
but it's March no leaves
no breeze just the score
for the scene
before me   silvery
glissandos rising
from a streaming swarm
of glinting
creatures herded
by the current
in a living touching
clinking singing surge

PROTEA WALKS THE RIVER

Deity of fog and snow-patched branch,
hooded markers, grillwork, and sun-
less sky, small ducks bobbing
and stars come down, the galaxies
in a statue's eyes.

Deity of haphazard hands, pilings, pumps,
and intake valves submerged
between the buoy and the shore.
Deity of no birds now and the silence
of ringing ears—can't you see how her path
is stodgy with snow?
                    Rootless as she has ever been,
won't you steady her, Deity—give her a sign?
We know you have been waiting for her
for a long, long time.

Protea, in Venice

Tonight she scorns the romantic
     fish   a flounder   built for two

The waves are risky   pulled
     by the moon   her hands

Can touch two walls   at once
     and her gaze   stretches forward

Then back   milk at the bottom of the sea
     seems less ludicrous   than before

O plowman   let her thumb through
     those cliff top ruins   gardens she raided

A ship in a storm on the sea   help her
     to understand   there will be safety

On the other side   spare her
     the lachrymose   conclusions.

PROTEA, HER TOWN

Decades break against sidewalks, alleys
once overgrown with roses and wild grapes.

She collected those baskets and books,
and a love never meant to rush faithfully

over the watershed and cruel fields, home
to crows and peregrines, now paved over brick by brick.

Beneath the moon's withdrawal from vanished
neighborhoods and gleaming canyons,

she toasts the living and the dead.
The rulers look down, unperturbed.

She came here, sight unseen,
the map only beginning to be drawn.

Even then she smelled smoke.
The crystals she examined for so long

still give a milky sheen
but do not tell the light.

III.

Again, the Moon

And now the moon, its *vitreous pour*
so quickly come again
moonstruck moon   melon moon

I drive the unfamiliar
town, going where Siri tells me
through unlit streets

I cannot dial back to another
moon, although there have been many—
moons of loss, lists, listing oh the self-
consciousness of the moon

Look at the moon in the sky,
not the one in the lake, says Rumi
The pleasures of heaven are with me
and the pains of hell are with me, says Whitman

So which is the lake and which
the sky? With a moon this bright
I cannot find the stars.

At Elmwood Cemetery:
The Cherry Now

for Deborah Thompson

Spring evening petals coat the headstones:
actual dates the anonymous
moss edges up against, a wooded
soundlessness the Hermit Thrush flits through,
lands, tilts atop the stone. How can I
not invoke, praise his pert endurance—
how he returns, tail bobbing, each year,
how star and storm know who we are. Praise
what is turbulent in its growing,
the viscous surfaces of the buds
glistening along each bough, coming
into blossom in the righteous light.

Palms I Have Known

I live in a state of limbo, one foot here, one foot there, torn between the river and the garden, the child and the children. I live in a state of perplexity, one foot in now and the other in then. Merwin showed me the way this morning, to absorb and loop and let all Being come through, at least that's what I think he is doing in *The Moon Before Morning*, feeling age and time and life as one continuum, one thrush could be any thrush, the one that sang and the one that sings, the mind of the palm-ist (thinking of his beloved trees) that looks up through fronds and sees the same sky. I look at my palm and consider the palms I have known. I have been annoyed at them recently, which is chastening and humbling to consider, in light of Merwin who does not overlay palms with meaning. I met him once, drove 80 miles to get there, exceeded the speed limit and was stopped by the police. I was living in the state of Ohio, coming from Michigan in a state of excitement and a state of oh what the hell throw caution to the etc...and the inevitable ticket. But there was Merwin, who really saw me, who gave me five minutes of his utterly undivided attention, a blessing like a palm frond waving, a kindness and a pure light I will never forget. Oh, the plants I did not water, the palm in its pot shedding its branches. I praise the potted palm for the way it takes up space in front of my window, imparting a kind of Victorian feeling to the room, though now it is waning, dry and brown along its fringes. Palm is a word that the auto dictation on my computer tries to give me instead of poem. It does not recognize poem. If it's not trying to turn a poem into a palm, it turns poem into problem. This might be something my friend Matt could handle deftly in a poem. Or Merwin, with pure simplicity. The simplicity of water poured from a wooden bucket under the filtered light coming down through the uppermost branches of a palm forest on the island of Maui.

W. S. Merwin (1927-2019)

WW, LOUNGING

Lounging in the grass, a wheatear at his lips, his beard ripe with sweat and sunlight, our Walt, WW, lister and lover, hears the river flowing not far away and the bare browned youths splashing there on the other side of the trees. He will be their conductor, their *drover*, the sparkle of their *regatta*, reclining now *with rigid head and just open'd lips*. His loins ache, his muscles begin to twitch. It doesn't matter that the ground holds him, his perfect silence the center of a great continental hum, crews and collectors, a history only beginning to be begun. What music does he hear but the song of self. Let's bring him forward, introduce him to, let's say, Ralph Cramden, waltzing through his sitcom. So, here's Walt, lounging with us all now, at the back door of the neighbor's house and in the boat tossed in the storm, the stable and the cave, and of course the sitcom. See him dance with Jackie Gleason, unrestrained, moving his bulk gracefully around the room. Or watch him break into break beat techno, or dodge and feint with brown bodies and basketballs out on the rez. Could he flip and rotate on his shoulder, spin on one arm or knee? Wherever we move, he moves, strong sweaty hairy man who cleans up well and wears sweetly laundered linen shirts as he dips and bows and settles down to *sit by the wounded and soothe them, or silently watch the dead.* He would make sure to smell good when he held their hands or gently closed their eyes, recalling with deep breaths his river and the grass and the young men who splashed and tussled and hugged, or that time when his limbs impelled him to move forward, remove those homespun garments, let lips press his breastbone, fingers stroke his beard, as he washed and splashed and embraced in the water and the sun.

OUTRIGGER

We are nine in the rented canoe
with many ages between us.
Danny, thirteen, takes the prow.
Five decades back on a small bench,
I sit behind Edwin, our guide,
whose paddle rises fine by the bank
whose voice sings encouragement and praise
who danced and laughed on the beach
and kicked a ball in the sand with the children
who showed me hummingbird chicks, their translucent
beaks barely reaching above the rim of their nest
spun like a cocoon at the end of its branch,
who found agouti and the Blue-crowned Motmot
and led my gaze up along the kapok's magnificent trunk.
And I sit behind him and raise my paddle
in rhythm with his paddle and turn my body
with weight from my waist and push down
into the waves when he does
and pull my arm back up again
and then we look up together
at soaring pelicans
and Magnificent Frigatebirds and I watch
little streams pour over his body.
There is no Frigate like a Book, I tell him
softly, from the seat behind,
but he doesn't hear me. He's already
looking *Lands away*, out, in the ocean,
me, aching to bathe by the shore.

FANGS, BEAK, AND FRUIT

after Neil Frankenhauser's "Water Color Critters"

Your giraffe leans from the top, looking into the swamp
below. No body, just neck and head craning in. You put a wash
of white over its orange face, a magenta shadow behind
one ear. And there goes an ocelot, hind quarters only, escaping

stage right, while a camel (is it?) looks up through heavily lidded,
half-opened eyes. Its nose, a vivid purple; the body yellow, striped red,
edged in green. Incisors, much too large for the mouth, protrude
like fangs. Were it to speak, it would lisp and slobber.

You probably thought you were finished with this piece,
but from the upper left a bright-eyed yellow angelfish pops in.
Innocent escapee from some balmy reef or neon aquarium,
will she thread her way through this cranky throng?

None of them—giraffe, birds, a weird pink foxish thing—
seems connected to the others except for the pale raven
you sent zooming in from the right, ready to bite the backside
of something with a beak that looks like it is already dead.

The eyes of emerging creatures, the eyes of evolution,
stare out at me from your river of writhing forms. Who knows
what time they tell? *Write. A. Poem. About. Me.* you wrote
on each face of the small packing box. I like that you like

that I liked what it contained, a wizened fruit
with bronzed leathery planes, mahogany crevices and gullies—
an apple perhaps, or pomegranate—that small cinnabar orb
you found in the back of your art closet and sent me.

Like this disappearing ocelot's shrinking penis,
it must have been plump once, fecund, smooth.
But now it's all angular surfaces, as if a giantess
inserted a straw and sucked out the pulp of it, and all the air.

Rooftop Flying in Ahmedabad

after the photo by Tal Streeter

They call it kite fever, kite madness, gangs of kite looting children
hoarding bright acid kites, darting through rows of kite kiosks,
until the kite wars of the Festival of Kites begin. One string must cut
another, the *Manjha*, the fighting string, fortified with a paste of spices,
rice, crushed glass and gems. *I felt I was being born again as a bird,*
says a boy of his virgin festival who ever after seeks that primal pull.
Bird or warrior? Bushad late to his wedding for lingering on the roof
flying kites, the sandalwood reel humming, his ring finger
clacking against the tug of flight. And what of our British photographer,
trekking the roiling Punjab to capture the eyes of God?
One of the self-styled *road trippers, track bashers...popping his head
out the bus window to soak in the gorgeous view,*
let him rain on us the hands of kite makers, parsimonious
vendors of kites, multicolored rice paste dyed and infused,
mythic kite creatures, kites hung with pennants and years ago—
so the story goes—a single gold wafer from the Mughul Nawab
that would fall into the arms of the one lucky man
in a crowd of thousands who could now support his family for a year.
Thus blessings waft down from a heaven full of dancing
symbols and backlit bamboo bones standing out in sunlight.
The rooftop bristles with men, but I, hidden woman
below the roof of the world—I will scribble secret kites,
contraband messages, the kind prisoners smuggle to those
beyond the bars. *Love me when I least deserve it,*
says my love, *because that is when I need it most.*
So I will not be a predatory kite, talons shadowing
the scouring light. I will say that in this grip of love I will be the best
prisoner I can be. Rapt by the wind-tossed chaos
of tug and go, clasp and ignore, I will expect no Aeolian hum to play
across my lines. I will make this a proper shield kite and keep my beloved
kiting always—kiting, yes, but never off, unlike my father's lifelong friend
on parasail whose heart gave out kiting swells of air.
Not *tako kichi*, kite crazy, let me stay small and humble
like a vendor who bundles kites in old papers tied with scraps of string.

A Wedding on the Island

with thanks to Hafiz

Not the stars themselves
but the spaces between them,
not the blades of the paddle
but their dip and rise and pull
through the water—think balance
and paradox, quixotic chime,
the way lovers, finding, recognize
each other, for *Only a Perfect One*
who is always laughing at the word Two
can make you know of love. Here
light becomes tangible, hovering
over and through our late summer
grasses. Milkweed, chicory, goldenrod
release their fragrances. Brisk
triangular sails move back and forth
on the horizon, tankers glide slowly
downstream, the glass domes glint
and gleam. What is a vow but a hope
and a prediction, a ring for memory, a song for luck.
Let *the myriad creatures grab their instruments*
and join the song. Scott and Lisa, seven
years is good number. You've had mountains
and music—and practice, practice—to build on.
Through you we see *life start clapping,*
learn how *whenever love makes itself known*
against another body, the jewel in the eye
starts to dance.

for Scott Boberg and Lisa Raschiatore
Belle Isle, Detroit
August 26, 2017

FLORIDA

for Neil

The dream tells me where I am:
nose close to a tulip tree
filled with lime green finches,
one that sports a spectacled mask
miming my every move. But here
all the palms look the same
and I am lost again in the parking lot
outside the hospital, searching
for my rental car, no stars,
no bearings, while across the planet
actual birds are falling from the sky.
At night I swim in the hotel pool
and look up past the trees. I have placed
the beach flotsam we gathered
next to the outdoor sink, said farewell
to sponge and seawrack,
and paid up the cottage and thrown away
the food we bought to move across town
into emergency housing. I have called
your children and sorted and shipped
your things and have ridden the elevator
up through the indoor atrium, past
the potted ficus trees and the pianist
playing holiday songs, and held firm
with the nurses and social workers
and moved your tray and adjusted the blinds,
the bed, and the television and watched
the TV until it was time to go.
I rode in the ambulance and
crossed the bridge and trembled in
the waiting room and met the doctors.
While they operated I drove out to the shore.
I walked the beach and picked up a shell.
I practiced the slow steps I knew would come
later, after they opened your heart.

IV.

And Somewhere a River

i.

A ball of wire supplants a body
Body of tangled knots of wire
The shirt ripped open to show
The street inside.

The dog that ran those streets
Still runs above the salt caverns,
Past cupolas and porches, rotundas--
And somewhere a river.

And somewhere a train, a track,
And somewhere tears. Numbness.
Custer's horse died. The piano
Player died, and the elevated train

Clattered above crowded streets.
Across the city the time-lapsed storm
Compressed and unloosed itself,
With wings extended, talons drawn.

ii.

With wings extended, talons drawn
A splayed, eroded bird lies flattened
On a distant island, primaries reaching
For currents to carry its screech

And soar, but now all flesh
And stench are scoured
Away. Essence of vanishing, etched
Almost like a fern on stone.

You poke, touch with tiny tongs
The bottle caps, flip-top cans, multi-
Colored string and fibers that refuse
Decay. Think treasure: trove un-

Covered, miscellaneous swag to adorn
An assemblage of flags, emblems
And bones the saw grass spikes have grown
Up and through and around.

iii.

Up and through and around
The forest with fingering wings
The eagle flew. You caught
The feathers' silhouette

Breathless, as if you had ridden
With him, crossed the crags
Or tumbled his fierce falls down.
Sign, or circumstance?

Niche or not, think who earlier
Trod here, silent, slippered
Through the grass at the bottom
Of the valley floor

And you somewhere, midway between
The(m)(n) and now, sky and soil,
Memory and erasure, the hu(man)
(Doc)ument unearthing.

iv.

Document. Unearthing
Past paths and phrases allows fugitive
Materials to make their way
Inside the frame. Ash. Clay.

Your life is happening
Without you now, raising a new
Surround of sound. Rust,
Inherently transitional, slides

In under the guise of stillness.
Wannabe escapee from this city
Of tomorrow, do you struggle
To maintain a pose? Your photograph

Will go on forever, drooping,
But then oddly resuming its position
In the abandoned car park
Under matted leaves and stems.

V.

Under matted leaves and stems
Afloat on the surface, the fathoms
Sound. Collect what you can,
Instructions nevertheless remain.

It is wet here, and dark. Yield, then.
It is important to listen: thrumming
Strings, incessant hum, each step
Bringing you closer to the river,

The ball, the bird and its outspread wings.

POEM IN OVERDRIVE

If too much honey clogs the arteries you travel
            & you brake for bromides, platitudes, each horn
honking its particular moral signature, the car radio whining
            all the common wisdoms you'd like to forget—
not getting any (younger, smarter, stronger) are we?
            Well then, don't say anything nice if you can't
say anything at all. Take it from me, I'm your dragon-baby,
            come to time the signs. I'm reborn more ways
than I can count & I'll tell you this: to make even a single teaspoon
            of homiletic tonic go down, it helps to remember the Universe
has not existed forever. In the midst of this *cammin di nostra vita*
            to surmount obstacles such as red lips screeching
like wheels taking a corner too fast or the skunky smog of Despair
            you roll your windows up against as you turn onto the drive
of the mansion of Self-pity, remind yourself that such disorder always
            increases with Time. Put Hope behind the mirror. Close
the door. If you take your face, that pear-shaped book, in your hands
            maybe then you'll read how your whole life has been
preparation for nothing more or less than this opportunity to dive into
            moments of infinite density where all your pasts collide
& your supposed self—that sieve of light—becomes scattered by
            matter many times. No sooner done than said, you say?
Then you're off, full drive, full gallop, posthaste, stir & stir alike, hustle,
            fuss, kick up a dust—push hard enough & you'll shift
into those zones whose vapors taste not as clouds of sorrow really
            but by-products of speed, Time's arrow pressing your pedal
to the floor. Top down, you'll dominate the passing lane. You'll be
            Emily Dickinson on her way out of town, whisking away
from Amherst or Tunis, whipping winds forcing moisture from your eyes
            —drops that will fall on your mother wit, mother tongue
only to leave Her far behind. You've always been completely self-contained,
            a point in Space or Time, but you're collapsing now, rushing
away from yourself the way galaxies do, into that elastic dark where
            background radiation's the same in all directions.

OSSAWA NIGHT

Il faut respecter le noir.
—Odilon Redon

if you could build a structure for the evening air
you would angle it such a way as to catch the last
cries of children counting rhymes   if you could
touch them   if you could sit endlessly counting
and listen to the throats of flowers opening
that moment   that singular note   which is not to retrace
another   ever   even in looking back you ascertain
the prow of a ship moving   the mindless sea
and the human form   soundless now as fish
                                        wave your hand
and they break soundless too those surfaces
oiled with the backs of them speckled faceless
as names wiped from stone   someone is
washing   lifting a corner of hem   wringing gentle
revelations   quick turns of leg   but there is   nothing
to reconsider
                        what if you never act upon the faith-
less future   end of self is itself felt as one   not
noose or loss   lift the garment again
five mute toes will always be there and the light
from whatever angle finding its way in

the landscape has hardened from your pastiche
of oils which have themselves landed in a harmless town where gates
turn inward and walls project shadows of olives
orchards   beards of elders   the braided hills   it is
here you sit on the parapet   your hand reaches
then returns as fishermen scrape their boats
against the sand   in another time   there would be nothing
but silhouettes here
                        you have accustomed yourself
to that thought and cast about in indigos and violets
for the best immutable shade

THE SADDLE: A MORPHOGENESIS

i. Imagine

Imagine a saddle, placed on the back of a horse with the felt pad underneath it, the stirrup hanging down. Imagine tightening the cinch a couple of extra notches after the horse stops holding in its breath and no longer expects it to be tightened, then placing your left foot in the stirrup and grabbing the pommel and pulling yourself up onto the top of the horse, throwing the right leg over and settling into the smooth leather and squeezing your thighs around it. Imagine, later, leaning forward and pushing your body loose from the saddle and flinging one leg over so you can slide comfortably to earth, the burnished, warm leather of the saddle against your chest. Imagine the reins and the horse with its mane falling to the right or left, and the warm withers and flanks of the animal you yearned to master and occasionally did, with long afternoon rides through the back pastures and fields, though more often it was a matter of falling, the saddle sliding loose, or the horse taking off with the bit in its teeth and a mind of its own. Why saddle? Where did it come from, floating up through the years, connecting one autumn to another, stored now in a barn on a rack or over the top of the stall, rubbed with saddle soap and shining through the fragrance of oats and the soft sounds of horses munching and snuffling and exhaling deep contented breaths. The ones who really know saddles and horses and stalls and gaits, who are they, who take the animal in hand, who give over all of their mind's attention to being with the beast? Who know the animals as individual beings, with quirks and habits and personalities? All the pretty little horses, your mother sang, coaxing you into animal worship and the pages that would open year after year with horses you would read about and later horses you would draw, sitting beside a tree outside the paddock where the yearlings were, so you could put them in your sketchbook. They were unsaddled at the time, and as young as you were, without saddles, unsaddled by all the years to come after.

ii. The Octo-Saddle

There were times when the saddle imagined it was an octopus, and in its imagining became an octopus, constraining its eight limbs into two stirrups and surreptitiously creeping out of the stable along the base of the stalls and into the evening air. Other days the saddle became a manta ray and lifted itself up and out through the windows in the largest stall and traveled through currents of air until it reached other saddle-rays to soar in a group over the wheat fields and along the edges of the forests, their stirrup appendages clacking against one another slightly because they preferred flying in close proximity and made of themselves a cloud. Humans living in the vicinity of these fields and forests could look up and see the cloud of saddle-rays swarming together and think, my the blackbirds are larger than usual this season and hear in the clacking of the stirrups the harsh clicks and caws of birds. When the saddle wanted to be alone, though, it snuck away as an octopus, moving against the edges of the stall and out the barn door, its leathery surface more fluid and malleable now, so it could meld in an embrace with a post or tree trunk and arrange its molecules accordingly, picking up the imprint of the bark or wooden surface so that if or when it resumed its saddle shape, there would be a texture to it, with markings like grooves on its surface that no saddle soap could wipe away. On these forays, the octo-saddle would try to dance. It picked up music from the thinnest vibrations in leaf cover, the low hum of mosses growing on abandoned stumps, the whispers of mushrooms pushing up through mulch and loam, and this music became a tune it hummed to itself as it made its way through the undergrowth or out into the fields past the barn. It moved like a ghost, a wraith, an ever-changing fog. When the moon rose in the evening, the octo-saddle would find a stationary spot and arrange itself there, with all the notes it held in its repertoire and compose them in greeting to the moon, softly at first and then in a crescendo as the moon rose higher into the sky.

NOT CROSSING BROOKLYN FERRY

Because the city// beyond the shore is no longer//
where we left it.
        —Ocean Vuong

I shall be an old woman
in seven syllables: here
the *udder of my heart*   there
        fog lowering over the
city I walked then the tops
of its high-rises para-
graphing up into layers
        of gray   mist and cloud   across
from this promenade lovers
mothers   children   dog-walkers
stroll   while over the water
        the surprise office escapes
surveillance   I lost its code
but not its elevator
or Alan who bulleted
        up in it with his scarf draped
rakishly round his rakish
neck   that mellow yellow year
Our Lady far off (there were
        songs about her, too) and small
The address a few blocks back
I found it again: 12 Hicks
decades elide   erasing
        data losing encryption
Therefore praise to the vendor
in the corner by the stairs
at the Clark St. subway stop
        still there   still giving the day
its one bright orgasm   loud
lush   fresh   primary petals
velvet textures   inside their
        garden   women   are singing
da do ron-ron-ron da do
        ron-ron but I   I came here

to take the air   to claim my
                own private Marienbad
I know less than ever now
          search others' eyes   scan the page
on the train   watch skyscrapers
          their disappearing syntax
awaiting passwords to cross
                    the border of—

In Her Chamber

Use the lead, long as you can,
thin mechanical (like steps)
going round. Through watery
panes the wavering pine wind
beginning to rock the toss
of shawl a shadow across
the bed now. Think sword, spear, shaft
                    of light.

                    No revelation
illumined watershed oh
welcome my muse anyhow
any angst-given moment.
Outside, ladder propped against
its apple tree father breeze
mother breeze winding the leaves.

Check list: candlestick, snuffer,
inkwell (glass, incised) books stacked
across the mantel with wild
Araby   Gib   innocent
in their frames. Maggie emptied
the commode placed water-filled
pans on the Franklin stove: steamed
to help her breathe. My larder
harder and harder to fill.

Come back come back oh maudlin
mind: here's a floor worn thin from
her tread yet original
and firm under rush matting.
Somewhere footfalls are: were: no
broken planks in reason. Yet.

Emily wine-haired woman
wintry sleigh bed night glider
did you sleep on your right or
your left? Did you hear lowing

from the road cowbells passing
in procession at sunset?

Check. Check again. Pleats neatly
spaced just above the white hem
a band of lace just below
the knee   a dozen buttons
climb to the throat wee and chaste
as Bombs you carried in your
Bosom wry sly with freedom
nigh likely to explode: here
at each click turn of your key.

Noon in a Corner Café: The Sign

We fix our eyes not on what is seen, but on what is unseen.
—2 Corinthians 4: 18

Not the angled
          umbrella   soft
conversation from a nearby table
               mutterings by the door...

Nor the mild air, a hibiscus
        there—or there, but something
closer.
               Noon now and its
rattle
         cups, traffic, taxis,
mopeds, their signature sounds.

     And what of
             the millions of hands
breaths, molecules
that have encountered
        my own.

         These stones
outlast us, pages
        picked up by

the breeze can say almost

anything, landing the way sunset
        falls over a pond

in the still woods, or over a shore,
        the one with a low dune

and a boy draping himself across it

in rapt abandonment to mist and sand
        and tide.

Call me mist dizzy   *the palpable...in its place*

                      One degree away.
Or another.

The sign
for infinity is a figure eight on its side.

                 She called it *noon*—
timeless palindrome, eternal place-
       holder—set its face-
         to-face *no*
              as a hinge   midway
down her lines where it would cast no
                  shadow.

                 Her room
looking west and south,
a modest corner, a room like any other, sun through the rippled glass,
                              the white dress
in its place   the moment
          you walk through the door.

Notes on the Poems

"Again, the Moon"—*vitreous pour* is from "Song of Myself, 21."

"Citizen Poet"— Italicized lines are from Sekou Sundiata's CD "The Blue Oneness of Dreams." "Space" was Sundiata's signature persona, a black-stream-of-consciousness, truth-telling monologist, a madman making mad sense of the world. Sundiata performed his "Space Monologue" at Dearborn's Arab American Museum in 2006 along with ten Detroit poets (this author included) for "This Poem has Checkpoints: A Concert of Poets." The concert culminated one of many "Lyrical Citizenship Post 9/11 Potlucks" that he convened nationwide in 2005-2006. For an appreciation of the beloved poet/activist, see "Sekou Sundiata, 1948-2007" by Vernon Reid, *www. villagevoice.com.*

"Down in Detroit"—For a discussion of this use of "default mode," see Toni Morrison, *Playing in the Dark.*

"The Extinct Freshwater Mussels of the Detroit River"—The extinct mussels' names are from an exhibit about invasive species at Detroit's Belle Isle Nature Center.

"ice music"—*Crumbling is not an instant's Act*, Emily Dickinson, (J)1010.

"In Her Chamber"—"But since we got a Bomb—/And held it in our Bosom—" Emily Dickinson, (J) 443.

"The Ivory Gull Under the Bridge over the Flint River"—Italicized lines from Whitman, "Song of Myself, 31." A "bird-while" is a term coined by Ralph W. Emerson to define the time one has to observe a bird on a branch before it flies off somewhere else.

"Noon in a Corner Café: the Sign"—*the palpable in its place* is from "Song of Myself, Section 16." According to Cynthia Griffin Wolff (*Emily Dickinson*, Knopf, 1986) the word *noon*, as both zero hour and eternity—a palindromic word of no's that has no beginning and no end—was key to "Dickinson's achievement of a fusion of infinity and nothingness." Precisely centered at the midpoint of over half a dozen poems, *noon* "serves the function of a sign created not by God but by the poet."

"Not Crossing Brooklyn Ferry"—*the udder of my heart* is from "Song of Myself, 28."

"One Less River"—Italicized lines from "A Rodeo Cowboy, Thrown by Life," *New York Times Magazine* (June 10, 2010).

"Ossawa Night" is in response to an exhibit of the works of Henry Ossawa Tanner.

"Outrigger"—*There is no Frigate like a Book*, Emily Dickinson (F) 1286.

"Palms I Have Known"—Matt refers to the inimitable Matthew Olzmann.

"Provincetown, August"—*Live frugally, on surprise* is from Alice Walker's "Expect Nothing." *Protea*, the author's coinage for a mythic female persona, is drawn from Proteus, a pre-Athenian Greek sea god. There appears to be no equivalent sea goddess.

"Rooftop Flying in Ahmedabad"—"Love me when I least deserve it..." is a Swedish proverb. Other quotations taken from *A Kite Journey through India* by Tal Streeter.

"She Awakens in a Town by the Sea"—*Mami Wata* (Mother Water) is a beautiful, protective, seductive, and dangerous water spirit celebrated throughout much of Africa and the African Atlantic. Mammatus refers to cloud formations that have the appearance of breasts.

"Stillness in the Air—Between"—From Emily Dickinson J(465) "I heard a Fly buzz..."

"Tallahatchie"—A Golden Shovel, the last words of this poem's lines are taken in order from Gwendolyn Brooks's "A Bronzeville Mother Loiters in Mississippi. Meanwhile, a Mississippi Mother Burns Bacon."

"A Wedding on the Island"—Italicized lines from Hafiz, "The Gift," translated by Daniel Ladinsky. "Quixotic chime" is from Anita Schmaltz.

"The Woodcock" samples "Song of Myself, 10," in which the speaker imagines succoring a run-away slave.

"WW, Lounging"—Whitman quotes are from "Song of Myself, 15" and "The Wound-dresser." This poem borrows from "Defending Walt Whitman" by Sherman Alexie.

AFTERWORD: THE RIVERS THAT REMAIN

By Keith Taylor

For several decades now I have thought of Terry Blackhawk as one of the writers central to the literary activity in Detroit. She taught in the public schools there and then established one of the essential Writers- in-the-Schools programs at InsideOut Literary Arts Project. The city has been proudly at the center of much of her work, particularly during those tough years before the place became fashionable once again with the young. See "Down in Detroit" here in *One Less River* for her scorn of those "who assume whiteness/unites" in their distaste and fear of the city.

But Terry Blackhawk has always refused to be pigeon-holed in one category. In addition to her portraits and celebrations of Detroit, her work has always been informed by her knowledge and appreciation of the natural world. Sometimes—and maybe its most interesting manifestation in this book—that world intrudes into or intersects with the city. The massive Detroit River, so important in our national history, flows into many of the poems in this book, including the gorgeous "ice music," where Blackhawk finds words for the sounds of the breakup of the ice on that cold torrent—"ice melt ice lace ice/breaking."

Detroit is, of course, an essentially American city. Its river defines one of the country's borders. Terry Blackhawk is comfortable claiming or reclaiming her country and its literary masters. She honors the influence of Emerson, Whitman and, essentially, Dickinson, and she enters into dialogue with them, filled with respect even when she might want to argue. She does this while she makes her associations with contemporary Detroit writers; the title poem of the book is an elegy for the poet and performer known by his first name, Blair, a dynamic presence in the life of Detroit before his tragic passing when he was only in his mid-40s.

The title, *One Less River*, and the epigraph from Hafiz ("As you mount the hidden tide and travel/Home") prepare us for the sense of loss that is in much of this book. And it is true; many of these poems celebrate or lament the things that are no longer there. They are indeed poems of aging. Yet the vividness of the perceptions, the strength of the language, and the willingness to engage difficult positions in our world, invigorate the poems and prepare us for all the work yet to come.

ABOUT THE AUTHOR

Dr. Terry Blackhawk is Founding Director (1995-2015) of Detroit's InsideOut Literary Arts Project (iO), a poets-in-schools program dedicated to encouraging young people to "think broadly, create bravely, and share their voices with the wider world." Blackhawk began writing poetry during her career as a Detroit high school teacher. She received the 1990 Foley Poetry Award, the 2010 Pablo Neruda Prize, the 2013 Springfed Arts Poetry Prize and grants from the National Endowment for the Humanities and Michigan Council for Arts and Cultural Affairs. Her poetry collections include *body & field* (Michigan State University Press, 1999), *Escape Artist* (BkMk Press, 2003), selected by Molly Peacock for the John Ciardi Prize; *The Dropped Hand* (2nd Edition, Lotus Press, imprint of WSU Press 2011); *The Light Between* (Wayne State University Press, 2012) and three chapbooks. Before her retirement, she co-edited *To Light a Fire: Twenty Years with the InsideOut Literary Arts Project* (WSU Press, 2015) with iO Senior Writer Peter Markus. The collection chronicles the growth of iO from her classroom teaching and features essays by writers who have brought the gift of poetry to children and youth in Detroit.

In addition to K-12 teaching, Blackhawk has taught creative writing pedagogy for graduate students at Oakland University and developed courses on ekphrastic writing that she taught on site at the Detroit Institute of Arts. She has a strong interest in Emily Dickinson and has presented at conferences and published essays and poems about the poet. She was twice named Creative Writing Educator of the Year by the Michigan Youth Arts Festival (1990, 2008) where she led the annual festival poetry workshop during the 1990s. Blackhawk was named a Kresge Arts in Detroit Literary Fellow in 2013. She holds a BA in Literature from Antioch College and a Ph.D. in Language Arts Education from Oakland University, which granted her an Honorary Doctorate in 2014. A long time Detroit resident and avid birder, she divides her time between Detroit and her family in Connecticut.

Acknowledgements

I extend sincere gratitude to the editors of the following publications in which these poems first appeared.

Black Renaissance Noire, 2016, Vol. 16, No.1. "Citizen Poet"

Cranbrook Review, 1990 *"Stillness in the Air—Between"*

Dispatch Detroit, 2002 "Ossawa Night"

Dunes Review, April 2018 "One Less River"; "Nauset"

Golden Shovel Anthology, University of Arkansas Press, 2017 "Tallahatchie"

Interim, 34:3, 2017 "The Extinct Freshwater Mussels of the Detroit River"; "The Ivory Gull Under the Bridge over the Flint River"; "Noon in a Corner Café: the Sign"

Interim, 35:3, 2018 "The Octo-saddle," "Imagine" (as "The Saddle")

The MacGuffin, Summer 2019, "Fangs, Beak, and Fruit," "Outrigger," "Overheard Among the Arthropods"

Michigan Quarterly Review: the Great Lakes, Love Song and Lament, 2011 "ice music"

New South Review, 2012 "Provincetown, August"

ONE, Issue 12, 2017 "She Awakens in a Town by the Sea"

The Peacock Journal, November 2016 "The Woodcock"

Peninsula Poets, 2012 "Protea Walks the River"

Poetry in Michigan, Michigan in Poetry, New Issues Press, 2013 "Down in Detroit"

River Oak Review, Winter 2002, "Poem in Overdrive"

Solstice, Summer/Fall 2014 "And Somewhere a River" (as "Unfinished Poem"), "Rooftop Flying in Ahmedabad"

Where are you from?: A Bilingual Anthology in English and Persian, 2017 "Grief, in Venice"; "Protea, Her Town"

"Florida" won First Place in the 2013 Springfed Arts Poetry Contest. Denise Duhamel, judge.

"Stillness in the Air—Between" also appeared in *Still Life with Conversation: a Dramatic Assemblage in Three Parts*, Ridgeway Press, 1993, Rebecca Emlinger Roberts, ed.

"Down in Detroit" also appeared in *A Detroit Anthology*, Rust Belt Press, 2014, Anna Clark, ed.

"The Octo-saddle" also appeared in *Purged*, by Nancy J. Rodwan, Ridgeway Press, 2018 (as "The Saddle: a Metamorphosis").

"The Woodcock" also appeared in *Where are you from?: A Bilingual Anthology in English and Persian*, Soodabeh Saiednia, ed ., 2017.

Some of these poems formed the script of "Protea Currency," a multi-genre poetic variety show featuring Detroit musicians, spoken word artists, and filmmakers at Wayne State's Studio Theater for the 2015 Detroit ArtX/ Kresge Arts Festival. Nancy J. Rodwan's film based on "Overheard Among the Arthropods" was also featured at Detroit's Scarab Club and the 2015 Mykonos Biennale. Links to this video and recordings of Marilyn Biery's settings of "Provincetown, August" and "Protea, in Venice" (on the 2018 CD "Poet as Muse: Music for Flute, Clarinet and Voice") can be found at *www. terrymblackhawk.com*. I am ever grateful to the Kresge Arts in Detroit program of the Kresge Foundation, which awarded me a 2013 Literary Fellowship as well as the grant that underwrote this creative collaboration.

Deepest thanks to the editors who brought these poems into the world and to the friends who have helped me understand them. To my first readers and responders: Kelly Fordon, Patricia Hooper, Peter Markus, Judy Michaels, Dunya Mikhail; to my partner-in-Whitman, Dennis Hinrichsen; to my lovely divas: Diane DeCillis, Lucinda Sabino, Joy Gaines Friedler, Nadia Ibrashi— your voices hover over these words. Special thanks to Charles Alexander, Lauren Hilger, Marie Howe, Ruth Padel, and Carl Phillips. Special thanks also to Soodabeh Saiednia for her elegant Farsi translations. And to Keith Taylor, for his photograph of the Ivory Gull and discovery of the "bird-while," gratitude for my appropriation.

Finally, thoroughgoing gratitude to Judith Kerman for her determination and care for these poems.

Other Recent Titles from Mayapple Press:

Ellen Cole, *Notes from the Dry Country, 2019*
        Paper, 88pp, $16.95 plus s&h
        ISBN 978-1-936419-87-6
Monica Wendel, *English Kills and other poems*
        Paper, 70pp, $15.95 plus s&h
        ISBN 978-1-936419-84-5
Charles Rafferty, *Something an Atheist Might Bring Up at a Cocktail Party*, 2018
        Paper, 40pp, $14.95 plus s&h
        ISBN 978-1-936419-83-8
David Lunde, *Absolute Zero*, 2018
        Paper, 82pp, $16.95 plus s&h
        ISBN 978-1-936419-80-7
Jan Minich, *Wild Roses*, 2017
        Paper, 100pp, $16.95 plus s&h
        ISBN 978-1-936419-77-7
John Palen, *Distant Music*, 2017
        Paper, 74pp, $15.95 plus s&h
        ISBN 978-1-936419-74-6
Eleanor Lerman, *The Stargazer's Embassy*, 2017
        Paper, 310pp, $18.95 plus s&h
        ISBN 978-936419-73-9
Dicko King, *Bird Years*, 2017
        Paper, 80pp, $14.95 plus s&h
        ISBN 978-936419-69-2
Eugenia Toledo, tr. Carolyne Wright, *Map Traces, Blood Traces /*
        Trazas de Mapas, Trazas de Sangre, 2017
        Paper, 138pp, $16.95 plus s&h
        ISBN 978-936419-60-9
Eric Torgersen, *In Which We See Our Selves: American Ghazals*, 2017
        Paper, 44pp, $14.95 plus s&h
        ISBN 978-936419-72-2
Toni Ortner, *A White Page Demands Its Letters*, 2016
        Paper, 40pp, $14.95 plus s&h
        ISBN 978-936419-70-8

For a complete catalog of Mayapple Press publications, please visit our website at *www.mayapplepress.com*. Books can be ordered direct from our website with secure on-line payment using PayPal, or by mail (check or money order). Or order through your local bookseller.